Introduction

The *Shiva Chalisa* is a revered devotional hymn dedicated to Lord Shiva, one of the principal deities in Hinduism, often referred to as the destroyer or transformer in the Holy Trinity (*Trimurti*) of Brahma, Vishnu, and Shiva. While Lord Brahma is the creator and Lord Vishnu the preserver, Lord Shiva is the deity who facilitates the destruction of the universe, creating space for renewal and regeneration. This cyclical process of creation, preservation, and destruction is considered essential to the cosmic balance.

The hymn, consisting of forty verses, extols Lord Shiva's divine qualities and attributes, recounts his stories and triumphs, and calls upon his blessings for protection, strength, wisdom, and spiritual liberation. It is believed that reciting the *Shiva Chalisa* with a sincere heart can invoke Shiva's mercy, helping one overcome obstacles, dispel negativity, and purify the mind and soul.

In the verses, Lord Shiva is often depicted as the ascetic, draped in ash, wearing the crescent moon upon his head, holding a trident, and accompanied by his beloved consort, Goddess Parvati, and their son, Lord Ganesha. Despite his terrifying form as *Rudra*, the destroyer, Lord Shiva is also recognized as the compassionate and benevolent deity, always ready to shower grace upon his devotees. Through the *Shiva Chalisa*, worshippers seek his divine intervention to alleviate suffering, grant wisdom, and offer solace in times of distress.

This powerful hymn is sung or chanted with deep reverence, especially on auspicious days like Mondays (*Somwar*), which are

Shiva Chalisa

Published in Sanskriti Press
by Rupa Publications India Pvt. Ltd 2025
7/16, Ansari Road, Daryaganj
New Delhi 110002

Sales centres:
Bengaluru Chennai
Hyderabad Jaipur Kathmandu
Kolkata Mumbai Prayagraj

Edition copyright © Rupa Publications India Pvt. Ltd 2025

All rights reserved.
No part of this publication may be reproduced, transmitted, or stored in a retrieval system, in any form or by any means, electronic, mechanical, photocopying, recording or otherwise, without the prior permission of the publisher.

P-ISBN: 978-93-5702-616-1
E-ISBN: 978-93-6156-913-5

Second impression 2025

10 9 8 7 6 5 4 3 2

Printed in India

This book is sold subject to the condition that it shall not, by way of trade or otherwise, be lent, resold, hired out, or otherwise circulated, without the publisher's prior consent, in any form of binding or cover other than that in which it is published.

dedicated to Lord Shiva, or during the festival of *Maha Shivaratri*. Each verse of the *Shiva Chalisa* serves as a reminder of Shiva's infinite powers and his immense mercy, and devotees often experience a sense of peace and spiritual upliftment after chanting it.

The *Shiva Chalisa* is not only a hymn of praise but a path to invoke divine blessings. Through its rhythm and repetition, it becomes a tool for meditation, helping practitioners to connect deeply with Lord Shiva and gain insight into the nature of life, death, and the cosmic order.

॥ दोहा ॥

जय गणेश गिरिजा सुवन, मंगल मूल सुजान ।
कहत अयोध्यादास तुम, देहु अभय वरदान ॥

Jai Ganesh Girija Suvan,
Mangal Mool Sujan.
Kahat Ayodhya Das Tum,
Dehu Abhay Vardan.

Glory to Lord Ganesha, son of Goddess Girija, the root of all auspiciousness and wisdom. Ayodhya Das requests you to grant the boon of fearlessness.

॥ चौपाई ॥

जय गिरिजा पति दीन दयाला ।
सदा करत सन्तन प्रतिपाला ॥

भाल चंद्रमा सोहत नीके ।
कानन कुंडल नागफनी के ॥

Jai Girija Pati Deen Dayala.
Sada Karat Santan Pratipala.
Bhal Chandrama Sohat Nike.
Kanan Kundal Nagphani Ke.

Glory to Lord Shiva, the consort of Goddess Girija and the compassionate savior of the distressed. He constantly protects saints and devotees. The crescent moon adorns his forehead beautifully, and his ears are graced with serpentine earrings.

अंग गौर शिर गंगा बहाये ।
मुण्डमाल तन छार लगाये ।।

वस्त्र खाल बाघम्बर सोहे ।
छवि को देख नाग मुनि मोहे ।।

Ang Gaur Shir Ganga Bahaye.
Mundamala Tan Chhaar Lagaye.
Vastra Khaal Baghambar Sohe.
Chhavi Ko Dekh Naag Muni Mohe.

His body glows white, and the sacred Ganga flows from his hair. He wears a garland of skulls and covers himself with ash. Draped in tiger skin, his divine appearance captivates sages and serpents alike.

॥ चौपाई ॥

मैना मातु की हवे दुलारी ।
वाम अंग सोहत छवि न्यारी ॥

कर त्रिशूल सोहत छवि भारी।
करत सदा शत्रुन क्षयकारी ॥

Maina Matu Ki Have Dulari.
Vam Ang Sohat Chhavi Nyari.
Kar Trishul Sohat Chhavi Bhari.
Karat Sada Shatrun Kshaykari.

Beloved daughter of Mother Maina, Goddess Parvati sits gracefully on Shiva's left side. The mighty trident in his hand enhances his imposing image, and he continually destroys the enemies of righteousness.

नन्दि गणेश सोहैं तहँ कैसे ।
सागर मध्य कमल हैं जैसे ॥

कार्तिक श्याम और गणराऊ।
या छवि को कहि जात न काऊ ॥

Nandi Ganesh Sohain Tahan Kaise.
Sagar Madhya Kamal Hain Jaise.
Kartik Shyam Aur Ganarau.
Ya Chhavi Ko Kahi Jat Na Kau.

Nandi and Lord Ganesh stand by his side, enhancing his majesty like lotuses blooming in an ocean. Kartikeya (Skanda) and the Ganas surround him, creating a divine scene that words cannot describe.

देवन जबहीं जाय पुकारा ।
तबही दुख प्रभु आप निवारा ।।

किया उपद्रव तारक भारी।
देवन सब मेली तुमहि जुहारी ।।

Devan Jabahi Jaya Pukara.
Tabahi Dukh Prabhu Aap Nivara.
Kiya Upadrav Tarak Bhari.
Devan Sab Meli Tumahi Juhari.

Whenever the gods call upon Lord Shiva for help, he immediately relieves their sufferings. When the demon Tarakasura caused great havoc, the gods united and sought refuge in him.

तुरत षडानन आप पठायउ ।
लव निमेष महँ मार गिरायउ ॥

आप जलंधर असुर संहारा ।
सुर यश तुम्हार विदित संसारा ॥

Turat Shadanana Aap Pathayau.
Lav Nimesh Mahin Maar Girayau.
Aap Jalandhara Asura Sanhara.
Sur Yash Tumhar Vidit Sansara.

Shiva promptly sent Kartikeya (Shadanana) to vanquish Tarakasura, who was slain in the blink of an eye. Similarly, he destroyed the demon Jalandhara, spreading his glory across the universe.

त्रिपुरासुर सन युद्ध मचाई ।
सबहि कृपा कर लीन बचाई ।।

किया तपहिं भागीरथ भारी ।
पुरव प्रतिज्ञा तासु पुरारी ।।

Tripurasur San Yudh Machai.
Sabahi Kripa Kar Leen Bachai.
Kiya Tapahin Bhagirath Bhari.
Purav Pratigya Tasu Purari.

Lord Shiva waged war against Tripurasura, protecting the gods through his grace. He also fulfilled Bhagiratha's penance by bringing the holy Ganga to Earth, keeping his divine promise.

दर्प छोड़ गंगा थब आई।
सेवक सुतस्तुति करत सदा ही ॥

वेद नाम महिमा तव गाई ।
अकथ अनादि भेद नहीं पाई ॥

Darp Chhod Ganga Tab Aayi.
Sevak Stuti Karat Sada Hi.
Ved Naam Mahima Tav Gai.
Akath Anadi Bhed Nahin Pai.

When Shiva released the Ganga from his locks, she descended to Earth, humbly abandoning her pride. Devotees constantly sing his praises, and the Vedas describe his greatness, though his infinite essence remains incomprehensible.

प्रकट उदधि मंथन में ज्वाला ।
जरत सुरासुर भए विहाला ॥

कीन्ही दया तहँ करी सहाई।
नीलकण्ठ तब नाम कहाई ॥

Pragat Udadhi Manthan Mein Jwala.
Jarat Surasur Bhaye Vihala.
Keenhi Daya Tahan Kari Sahayee.
Neelkanth Tab Naam Kahai.

During the churning of the ocean, a deadly poison emerged, terrifying both the gods and demons. Out of compassion, Lord Shiva drank the poison to save the universe, earning the name Neelkanth (the blue-throated one).

पूजन रामचन्द्र जब कीन्हा ।
जीत के लंक विभीषण दीन्हा ॥

सहस कमल में हो रहे धारी।
कीन्ह परीक्षा तबहि पुरारी ॥

Pujan Ramchandra Jab Kinha.
Jeet Ke Lanka Vibhishan Dinha.
Sahas Kamal Mein Ho Rahe Dhari.
Kinha Pariksha Tabahi Purari.

When Lord Ram performed Shiva's worship, he emerged victorious and handed over Lanka to Vibhishan. Shiva once tested Ram's devotion by concealing a lotus meant for worship, compelling Ram to offer one of his lotus-like eyes instead.

एक कमल प्रभु राखेउ जोई ।
कमल नयन पूजन चाहैं सोई ॥

कठिन भक्ति देखी प्रभु शंकर ।
भए प्रसन्न दिए इच्छित वर ॥

Ek Kamal Prabhu Rakheu Joi.
Kamal Nayan Pujan Chahain Soi.
Kathin Bhakti Dekhi Prabhu Shankar.
Bhaye Prasanna Diye Ichchhit Var.

When only one lotus remained, Lord Ram, known as Kamalnayan (lotus-eyed), offered his eye as the final lotus. Impressed by such unwavering devotion, Shiva granted Ram his desired boon.

जय जय जय अनंत अविनाशी ।
करत कृपा सबके घटवासी ॥

दुष्ट सकल नित मोहि सतावै ।
भ्रमत रहौं मन चौन न आवै ॥

Jai Jai Jai Anant Avinashi.
Karat Kripa Sabke Ghatvasi.
Dusht Sakal Nit Mohi Satavai.
Bhramat Rahun Man Chain Na Aavai.

Glory to the eternal and indestructible Lord Shiva, who resides in the hearts of all and showers his grace upon them. The wicked trouble me constantly, leaving my mind restless and unsettled.

त्राहि त्राहि मैं नाथ पुकारो ।
यहि अवसर मोहि आन उबारो ।।

लै त्रिशूल शत्रुन को मारो ।
संकट से मोहि आन उबारो ।।

Trahi Trahi Main Nath Pukaro.
Yahi Avasar Mohi Aan Ubaro.
Lai Trishul Shatrun Ko Maro.
Sankat Se Mohi Aan Ubaro.

O Lord, I cry out to you for help. At this moment, I beseech you to rescue me. Wield your trident to destroy my enemies and deliver me from this great crisis.

मात पिता भ्राता सब होई ।
संकट में पूछत नहीं कोई ।।

स्वामी एक है आस तुम्हारी।
आय हरहु अब संकट भारी ।।

Mata Pita Bhrata Sab Hoi.
Sankat Mein Poochat Nahin Koi.
Swami Ek Hai Aas Tumhari.
Aay Harahu Ab Sankat Bhari.

In times of distress, even close relatives like parents and siblings do not stand by me. You are my sole refuge, O Lord. Please come and alleviate my severe troubles.

धन निर्धन को देत सदा ही ।
जो कोई जाँचौ सो फल पाही ।।

अस्तुति केहि विधि करौं तुम्हारी।
शम्भु नाथ अब टेक तुम्हारी ।।

Dhan Nirdhan Ko Det Sada Hi.
Jo Koi Jaanchhe So Phal Pahi.
Astuti Kehi Vidhi Karon Tumhari.
Shambhu Nath Ab Tek Tumhari.

Lord Shiva provides wealth to the poor and fulfills the desires of those who seek his blessings. I am at a loss for words to praise your greatness and depend entirely on your mercy.

शंकर हो संकट के नाशन ।
मंगल कारण विघ्न विनाशन ॥

योगी यति मुनि ध्यान लगावैं।
सारद नारद शीश नवावैं ॥

Shankar Ho Sankat Ke Nashan.
Mangal Karan Vighn Vinashan.
Yogi Yati Muni Dhyan Lagavan.
Sharad Narad Shish Navavan.

O Shankar, the destroyer of all troubles and obstacles, you bring auspiciousness to all. Sages, ascetics, and devotees meditate upon you, while Narad and Saraswati bow their heads in reverence.

नमो नमो जय नम: शिवाय ।
सुर ब्रह्मादिक पार न पाय ॥

जो यह पाठ करे मन लाई।
ता पर होत है शम्भु सहाई ॥

Namo Namo Jai Namah Shivaya.
Sur Brahmadik Par Na Paya.
Jo Yah Path Kare Man Layi.
Ta Par Hot Hai Shambhu Sahayee.

I bow repeatedly to Lord Shiva, whose glory even gods like Brahma cannot fathom. Those who recite this Chalisa with devotion are always supported and blessed by Lord Shiva.

ऋणिय जो कोई हो अधिकारी ।
पाठ करे सो पावन हारी ।।

पुत्र हीन इच्छित कर कोई।
निश्चय शिव प्रसाद तेहि होई ।।

Riniya Jo Koi Ho Adhikari.
Path Kare So Pavan Hari.
Putra Heen Ichchhit Kar Koi.
Nischay Shiva Prasad Tehi Hoi.

Those burdened with debts and responsibilities can be freed by reciting this Chalisa. Even those yearning for a child will have their wish granted through Lord Shiva's grace.

पण्डित त्रयोदशी को लावे ।
ध्यान पूर्वक होम करावे ।।

त्रयोदशी व्रत करे हमेशा।
ताके तन नहीं रहे कलेशा ।।

Pandit Trayodashi Ko Lavai.
Dhyan Purvak Hom Karavai.
Trayodashi Vrat Kare Hamesha.
Take Tan Nahin Rahe Kalesha.

Invite a learned priest on the occasion of Trayodashi and perform sacred rituals with devotion. Observing the Trayodashi fast regularly ensures that one's body remains free of afflictions and distress.

धूप दीप नैवेद्य चढ़ावे ।
शंकर सम्मुख पाठ सुनावे ॥

जन्म जन्म के पाप नसावे।
अंत धाम शिवपुर में पावे ॥

Dhoop Deep Naivedya Chadhave.
Shankar Sammukh Path Sunave.
Janma Janma Ke Paap Nasave.
Ant Dham Shivpur Mein Pave.

Offer incense, lamps, and food to Lord Shiva while reciting this Chalisa in his presence. This destroys the sins of countless lifetimes and ensures that one attains liberation in Lord Shiva's divine abode.

॥ दोहा ॥

नित्य नियम उठि प्रातः ही ।
पाठ करो चालीसा ॥

तुम मेरी मनोकामना ।
पूर्ण करो जगदीश ॥

Nitya Niyam Uthi Pratah Hi.
Path Karo Chalisa.
Tum Meri Manokamna.
Purna Karo Jagdish.

Begin each day with discipline and devotion by reciting this Chalisa early in the morning. Lord Shiva, please fulfill my heartfelt desires.

मगसर छठि हेमन्त ऋतु ।
संवत चौसठ जान ॥

स्तुति चालीसा शिवहि।
पूर्ण कीन कल्याण ॥

Magsar Chhathi Hemant Ritu.
Samvat Chousath Jaan.
Stuti Chalisa Shivahi.
Purn Keen Kalyaan.

On a winter day during the Magsar month, this Chalisa was composed to praise Lord Shiva and bring fulfillment and well-being to his devotees.

॥ श्री शिव चालीसा सम्पूर्ण ॥

||Shri Shiva Chalisa Sampurna||

Thus, ends the Shiva Chalisa

||शिवाष्टक||

जय शिव शंकर, जय गंगाधर, करुणाकर करतार हरे,
जय कैलाशी, जय अविनाशी, सुखराशि सुखसार हरे,
जय शशि शेखर, जय डमरूधर, जय जय प्रेमागार हरे,
जय त्रिपुरारी, जय मदहारी, अमित, अनन्त, अपार हरे,
निर्गुण जय जय, सगुण अनामय, निराकार साकार हरे,
पारवती पति हर हर शम्भो, पाहि पाहि दातार हरे ।।1।।

Jai Shiv Shankar, Jai Gangadhar,
Karunakaar Kartar Hare,
Jai Kailashi, Jai Avinashi, Sukhrashi
Sukhsaara Hare,
Jai Shashi Shekhar, Jai Damrudhar,
Jai Jai Premagaar Hare,
Jai Tripuraari, Jai Madhari,
Amit, Anant, Aapaar Hare,
Nirgun Jai Jai, Sagun Anaamaya,
Niraakaar Saakaar Hare,
Parvati Pati Har Har Shambho, Paahi
Paahi Daatar Hare ||1||

Hail to Lord Shiva, the Lord of Ganga,
the compassionate creator,
Hail to the one who resides in Kailash,
the imperishable, the source of
joy and bliss,
Hail to the moon-crowned one, the one
who holds the damru (drum),
the abode of love,
Hail to Tripuraari, the vanquisher of
demons, the infinite and
immeasurable one,
You who are both formless and with form,
without attributes and with attributes,
O husband of Parvati, Hail to you, the
bestower of blessings!

जय रामेश्वर, जय नागेश्वर, वैद्यनाथ, केदार हरे,
मल्लिकार्जुन, सोमनाथ जय, महाकाल ओंकार हरे,
त्रयम्बकेश्वर, जय घुश्मेश्वर, भीमेश्वर, जगतार हरे,
काशी पति श्री विश्वनाथ जय, मंगलमय, अघहार हरे,
नीलकण्ठ जय, भूतनाथ जय, मृत्युञ्जय अविकार हरे,
पारवती पति हर हर शम्भो, पाहि पाहि दातार हरे ।।2।।

Jai Rameshwar, Jai Nageshwar,
Vaidyanath, Kedar Hare,
Mallikarjun, Somnath Jai,
Mahakal Omkar Hare,
Trayambakeshwar, Jai Ghushmeshwar,
Bhimeshwar, Jagatar Hare,
Kashi Pati Shri Vishwanath Jai,
Mangalmaya, Aghahaar Hare,
Neelkanth Jai, Bhutnath Jai, Mrityunjay
Avikaar Hare,
Parvati Pati Har Har Shambho, Paahi
Paahi Daatar Hare ||2||

Hail to Lord Rameshwar, the Lord of
Serpents, the healer and the
Lord of Kedarnath,
Hail to the one who resides at Mallikarjun
and Somnath, the Mahakal, the Omkara,
Hail to Trayambakeshwar, the one at
Ghusmeshwar, the one who
protects the universe,
Hail to the Lord of Kashi, Lord
Vishwanath, the one who
removes all obstacles,
Hail to the one with a blue
throat, the Lord of spirits, the
one who conquers death,
O husband of Parvati, Hail to you,
the bestower of blessings!

जय महेश, जय जय भवेश,
जय आदिदेव, महादेव विभो,
किस मुख से हे गुणातीत,
प्रभु तव अपार गुण वर्णन हो,
जय भवकारक, तारक,
हारक, पातक-दारक शिव शम्भो,
दीन दु:खहर, सर्व सुखाकर,
प्रेम-सुधाधर दया करो,
पार लगा दो भवसागर से,
बन कर कर्णाधार हरे,
पारवती पति हर हर शम्भो,
पाहि पाहि दातार हरे ।।3।।

*Jai Mahesh, Jai Jai Bhavesh, Jai Aadi Dev,
Mahadev Vibho,
Kis Mukh Se He Gunateet, Prabhu Tava
Apara Gun Varnan Ho,
Jai Bhavkaarak, Taarak, Haark, Paathak-
Daark Shiv Shambho,
Deen Dukhhar, Sarv Sukhakar, Prem-
Sudhadhar Daya Karo,
Paar Laga Do Bhavasagar Se, Ban Kar
Karnadhara Hare,
Parvati Pati Har Har Shambho, Paahi
Paahi Daatar Hare ॥3॥*

Hail to Mahesh, the Lord of the universe,
the primordial God, the great and powerful,
How can we describe your immeasurable
qualities, O Lord, who transcend
all attributes?
Hail to the creator, the savior, the
remover of sins, the purifier of the soul,
You who relieve the suffering of the poor
and bring all happiness, shower your mercy,
Guide us across the ocean of worldly
existence, O support of the universe,
O husband of Parvati, Hail to you, the
bestower of blessings!

जय मनभावन, जय अतिपावन,
शोक नशावन शिवशम्भो,
विपद विदारन, अधम उबारन,
सत्य सनातन शिवशम्भो,
सहज वचनहर, जलज नयनवर,
धवल-वरन-तन शिवशम्भो,
मदन-कदन-कर, पाप-हरन-हर,
चरन-मनन-धन शिवशम्भो,
विवसन, विश्वरूप, प्रलयंकर,
जग के मूलाधार हरे,
पारवती पति हर हर शम्भो,
पाहि पाहि दातार हरे ।।4।।

Jai Manbhavan, Jai Atipavan,
Shok Nashavan Shivshambho,
Vipad Vidharn, Adham Ubaarn,
Satya Sanatan Shivshambho,
Sahaj Vachanhar, Jalaj Nayanvar,
Dhaval-Varan-Tan Shivshambho,
Madan-Kadan-Kar, Paap-Haran-Har,
Charan-Manan-Dhan Shivshambho,
Vivasan, Vishwaroop, Pralayankar,
Jag Ke Mooladhar Hare,
Parvati Pati Har Har Shambho,
Paahi Paahi Daatar Hare ॥4॥

Hail to the one who delights the heart,
the one who purifies and removes sorrow,
The one who removes all obstacles, the savior of the fallen, the eternal truth,
You who speak gently, whose eyes are like lotus flowers, with a white and glowing form,
You who destroy passion, remove sins, and purify through your feet,
mind, and wealth,
You are the one who transcends the world, the form of the universe, the foundation of the world,
O husband of Parvati, Hail to you, the bestower of blessings!

भोलानाथ कृपालु, दयामय,
औढरदानी शिवयोगी,
निमिष मात्र में देते हैं,
नव निधि मनमानी शिवयोगी,
सरल हृदय, अति करुणा सागर,
अकथ कहानी शिवयोगी,
भक्तों पर सर्वस्व लुटाकर,
बने मसानी शिवयोगी,
स्वयं अकिंचन, जन मन रंजन,
पर शिव परम उदार हरे,
पारवती पति हर हर शम्भो,
पाहि पाहि दातार हरे ।।5।।

Bholanath Kripalu, Dayamaya,
Audhardani Shiv Yogi,
Nimish Matra Mein Dete Hai,
Nav Nidhi Manmaani Shiv Yogi,
Saral Hriday, Ati Karuna Sagar,
Akath Kahani Shiv Yogi,
Bhakton Par Sarvasva Lutakar,
Bane Masani Shiv Yogi,
Swayam Akinchana, Jan Man Ranjan,
Par Shiv Param Udaar Hare,
Parvati Pati Har Har Shambho,
Paahi Paahi Daatar Hare ||5||

Hail to the merciful Bholanath,
the ocean of compassion, the giver
of divine knowledge,
In the blink of an eye, he grants the
treasure of the heart's desire,
the unselfish one,
With a simple heart, the ocean of mercy,
whose stories cannot be fully described,
He gives everything to his devotees,
becoming the one with divine knowledge,
Selfless, the source of joy for all, the most
generous and compassionate,
O husband of Parvati, Hail to you, the
bestower of blessings!

आशुतोष ! इस मोहमयी निद्रा से मुझे जगा देना,
विषम वेदना से विषयों की मायाधीश छुड़ा देना,
रूप सुधा की एक बूंद से जीवन मुक्त बना देना,
दिव्य ज्ञान भण्डार युगल चरणों में लगन लगा देना,
एक बार इस मन मन्दिर में कीजे पद संचार हरे,
पारवती पति हर हर शम्भो, पाहि पाहि दातार हरे ।।6।।

Ashutosh! Is Mohamayi
Nidra Se Mujhe Jaga Dena,
Visham Vedana Se Vishayon
Ki Mayaadhish Chhuda Dena,
Roop Sudha Ki Ek Boond
Se Jeevan Mukt Bana Dena,
Divya Gyaan Bhandaar Yugal
Charanon Mein Lagan Laga Dena,
Ek Baar Is Man Mandir Mein
Keeje Pad Sanchar Hare,
Parvati Pati Har Har Shambho,
Paahi Paahi Daatar Hare ||6||

O Ashutosh! Wake me from this
illusionary sleep,
Liberate me from the pain of material
desires and their illusions,
With a single drop of the nectar of your
form, grant me liberation,
Fill my heart with divine knowledge and
devotion at your sacred feet,
Once, step into this temple
of my mind, O Lord,
O husband of Parvati, Hail to you, the
bestower of blessings!

दानी हो, दो भिक्षा में, अपनी
अनपायनी भक्ति प्रभो,
शक्तिमान हो, दो अविचल
निष्काम प्रेम की शक्ति प्रभो,
त्यागी हो, दो इस असार-संसार
से पूर्ण विरक्ति प्रभो,
परम पिता हो, दो तुम अपने
चरणों में अनुरक्ति प्रभो,
स्वामी हो, निज सेवक की
सुन लेना करुण पुकार हरे,
पारवती पति हर हर शम्भो,
पाहि पाहि दातार हरे ।।7।।

*Daanee Ho, Do Bhiksha Mein, Apni
Anpaayanee Bhakti Prabho,
Shaktimaan Ho, Do Avichal Nishkaam
Prem Ki Shakti Prabho,
Tyaagi Ho, Do Is Asar-Sansar Se Poorn
Virakti Prabho,
Param Pita Ho, Do Tum Apne Charanon
Mein Anurakti Prabho,
Swami Ho, Nij Sevak Ki Sun Lena Karun
Pukaar Hare,
Parvati Pati Har Har Shambho, Paahi
Paahi Daatar Hare ||7||*

O Lord, the giver of charity, bless me
with your infinite devotion,
O all-powerful one, bestow upon me the
unshakable power of selfless love,
O renouncer, grant me complete
detachment from this illusory world,
O Supreme Father, instill in me
attachment to your divine feet,
O Lord, listen to the compassionate plea
of your servant,
O husband of Parvati, Hail to you, the
bestower of blessings!

तुम बिन 'बेकल' हूँ प्राणेश्वर,
आ जाओ भगवन्त हरे,
चरण शरण की बांह गहो,
हे उमा-रमण प्रियकन्त हरे,
विरह-व्यथित हूँ, दीन दुःखी हूँ,
दीन-दयालु अनन्त हरे,
आओ तुम मेरे हो जाओ,
आ जाओ श्रीमन्त हरे,
मेरी इस दयनीय दशा पर,
कुछ तो करो विचार हरे,
पारवती पति हर हर शम्भो,
पाहि पाहि दातार हरे ।।8।।

Tum Bin 'Bekal' Hoon Praneshwar,
Aa Jao Bhagwant Hare,
Charan Sharan Ki Baah Gaho,
He Uma-Raman Priyakanth Hare,
Virah-Vyathit Hoon, Deen Dukhee Hoon,
Deen-Dyaalu Anant Hare,
Aao Tum Mere Ho Jao,
Aa Jao Shreemant Hare,
Meri Is Dayaneey Dasha Par,
Kuch To Karo Vichaar Hare,
Parvati Pati Har Har Shambho,
Paahi Paahi Daatar Hare ||8||

Without you, O Lord of life, I am
helpless, please come, O Lord,
Take me in the embrace of your feet, O
beloved consort of Uma,
I am tormented by separation, I am poor
and afflicted, O infinite merciful one,
Come to me, make me yours, come O
most prosperous one,
Please show compassion for
my pitiable state,
O husband of Parvati, Hail to you, the
bestower of blessings!

नम: शम्भवाय च मयोभवाय च नम: शङ्काराय च,
मयस्कराय च नम: शिवाय च शिवतराय च ॥

Namah Shambhavaay Cha Mayobhavaay
Cha Namah Shankaraay Cha,
Mayaskaraay Cha Namah Shivaay Cha
Shivtaraay Cha

Salutations to Shambhu (Lord Shiva), to the one who is beyond birth and death,
Salutations to Shankara, the one who removes all obstacles,
Salutations to Shiva, the supreme consciousness, the best of all!

शिव आरती

ॐ जय शिव ओंकारा स्वामी जय शिव ओंकारा ।
ब्रह्मा विष्णु सदा शिव अर्द्धांगी धारा ॥
॥ ॐ जय शिव ओंकारा ॥

एकानन चतुरानन पंचानन राजे ।
हंसानन गरुड़ासन वृषवाहन साजे ॥
॥ ॐ जय शिव ओंकारा ॥

दो भुज चार चतुर्भुज दस भुज अति सोहे ।
त्रिगुण रूपनिरखता त्रिभुवन जन मोहे ॥
॥ ॐ जय शिव ओंकारा ॥

अक्षमाला बनमाला रुण्डमाला धारी ।
चंदन मृगमद सोहै भाले शशिधारी ॥
॥ ॐ जय शिव ओंकारा ॥

श्वेताम्बर पीताम्बर बाघम्बर अंगे ।
सनकादिक गरुणादिक भूतादिक संगे ॥
॥ ॐ जय शिव ओंकारा ॥

कर के मध्य कमंडलु चक्र त्रिशूल धर्ता ।
जगकर्ता जगभर्ता जगसंहारकर्ता ॥
॥ ॐ जय शिव ओंकारा ॥

ब्रह्मा विष्णु सदाशिव जानत अविवेका ।
प्रणवाक्षर मध्ये ये तीनों एका ।।
।। ॐ जय शिव ओंकारा ।।

काशी में विश्वनाथ विराजत नन्दी ब्रह्मचारी ।
नित उठि भोग लगावत महिमा अति भारी ।।
।। ॐ जय शिव ओंकारा ।।

त्रिगुण शिवजीकी आरती जो कोई नर गावे ।
कहत शिवानन्द स्वामी मनवांछित फल पावे ।।
।। ॐ जय शिव ओंकारा ।।

Shiva Aarti

Om Jai Shiv Omkara
Swami Jai Shiv Omkara.
Brahma Vishnu Sada
Shiv Ardhangi Dhara.
Om Jai Shiv Omkara.

Ekanan Chaturanan Panchanan Raaje.
Hansanan Garudasana Vrishavahan Saaje.
Om Jai Shiv Omkara.

Do Bhuj Char Chaturbhuj
Das Bhuj Ati Sohe.
Trigun Roopnirakhta Tribhavan Jan Mohe.
Om Jai Shiv Omkara.

Akshamala Banmala Rundmala Dhaari.
Chandan Mrigmad Sohai Bhaale Shashidhari.
Om Jai Shiv Omkara.

Shvetambar Peetambar Baaghambar Ange.
Sanakadik Garunadik Bhutadik Sange.
Om Jai Shiv Omkara.

Kar Ke Madhya Kamandalu Chakra Trishul Dharta.
Jagakarta Jagbharta Jagsanharakarta.
Om Jai Shiv Omkara.

Brahma Vishnu Sadaashiv Jaant Aviveka.
Pranavakshar Madhye Ye Teenon Eka.
Om Jai Shiv Omkara.

Kashi Mein Vishwanath Virajat Nandi Brahmachaari.
Nit Uthi Bhog Lagawat Mahima Ati Bhaari.
Om Jai Shiv Omkara.

Trigun Shivji Ki Aarti Jo Koi Nar Gaave.
Kahat Shivanand Swami Manwanchhit Phal Paave.
Om Jai Shiv Omkara.